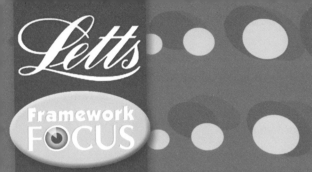

Letts

Framework FOCUS

YEAR

8

Spelling

Louis Fidge
Ray Barker

How to use this book

Letts Framework Focus: Spelling books have been designed to provide a versatile resource, capable of being used for a variety of teaching and learning situations and by a wide range of teachers – specialists and non-specialists alike. They:

- contain 30 units of work, sufficient for one school year
- are straightforward and easy to use
- provide discrete double-page spread format for quick reference
- have a clear teaching focus
- contain differentiated activities for each objective.

Letts Framework Focus: Spelling books can be used in a variety of ways:

- They easily provide work for the whole class, groups or individuals.
- Use them to introduce a key literacy topic – as a lesson 'starter'.
- The structure of the pages allows for teaching a particular literacy issue to the whole class.
- Units allow teachers to focus on a particular issue if this seems a problem for an individual or group.
- Planned progression allows teachers to consolidate, develop and extend literacy work over the year.
- Each unit provides work for follow-up homework assignments.

As a lesson starter

The Spelling Focus provides a clear explanation of each objective with examples for discussion or illustration. Appropriate activities may be chosen from the range of differentiated tasks for discussion, or to work through with the class.

Group and individual work

These books are ideal for group and individual work. Teaching on the same subject can be realistically matched appropriately to individual pupils' abilities, allowing pupils to work independently.

Homework

The design of the material in the books provides an ideal solution to meaningful homework assignments – differentiated appropriately for each pupil.

Contents Year 8 Spelling

Objective ·····❯

- To explore spelling patterns of some consonants and formulate rules.

Spelling Focus 📄

- Letters can be divided into vowels and consonants. The vowels are a, e, i, o, u. The rest of the letters of the alphabet are consonants.

- It is useful to recognise when consonants are pronounced in a **hard** or a **soft** way. For example, the 'g' in *'guitar'* sounds hard; the 'g' in *'general'* sounds soft.

- When you add 'full' or 'all' to the beginning or the ending of a word, one of the final consonants of the suffix or prefix is dropped.

  I am full of hope. I am hopeful.

- Single-syllable words ending in a consonant which is preceded by one vowel double their last letter when suffixes such as 'ing', 'er' or 'ed' are added.

Starter ❯

❶ Look at the words below.
Find any words you do not understand in a dictionary.

> guitar, gymnasium, guess, great, tongue, general, plague, gold, genius, goalkeeper, gesture, generous, gist, grasp, gangrene, gum, gash, gypsy, ghost

Copy and complete the chart by deciding whether the words use hard or soft consonants.

Hard consonant 'g'	Letter(s) immediately following it	Soft consonant 'g'	Letter(s) immediately following it
guitar	u		

❷ Using the results from your investigation write some rules about when the consonant 'g' is hard or soft .

Practice »

3 Add the suffix 'full' to these words. Check your answers in a dictionary.

(a) hope
(b) joy
(c) play
(d) thank   + full
(e) hate
(f) cheer
(g) tear
(h) spoon

4 Add the prefix 'all' to these words. Check your answers in a dictionary.

(a) ready   (d) though
(b) ways   (e) most
(c) together

5 Explain what happens to the spelling of the prefix and suffix when you word build.

Extension »»

6 Add 'ing', 'er' and 'ed' to these words where possible.

(a) rob   (d) hum   (g) wheel   (j) hop
(b) dot   (e) fail   (h) shine
(c) slim   (f) cool   (i) hope

REMEMBER

You will not have a double consonant without a vowel in front of it.

7 Check how many syllables the root words contain.
Look closely at the last letter of the root word.
Look at the letters before the final letter.
Write a rule about when to double the final consonant.

8 Try doing the same with: travel, patrol, marvel.
What do you notice?
Check your spelling in a dictionary.

Feedback ↩

When you add the suffix 'full' to a word, you always lose the final 'l'. When you add 'all' as a prefix to a word, you will also lose the final 'l'.

Single-syllable words ending in a consonant which is preceded by one vowel double their last letter when suffixes such as 'ing', 'er' or 'ed' are added.

Unit 2: Doubling consonants

Objective •••••>

- To consolidate conventions and spelling rules.

Spelling Focus

- Words involving double letters can be tricky to spell.

  hop – hopping? hoping?

  In this unit you will find some rules which can help you. However, there are other ways in which you can understand where double letters go in words.

- Try saying the word in certain ways – in rhythm, like a chant, stressing certain letters.

  neCeSSary

- Try remembering the shape of a word.

  dis appear

- Try sounding out its syllables.

  to / mor / row

Starter >

1 Add 'ing' to these single-syllable words.
Write out the words.
Check your spelling in a dictionary.

- (a) hop
- (b) rob
- (c) dig
- (d) skip
- (e) swim
- (f) shop
- (g) fit
- (h) hum

+ ing

2 Look at your answers to the last question.
Copy and complete this rule:

When you add a suffix to the end of a single-syllable word which has a single vowel before the final consonant _____.

Practice >>

3 Write out the words.
Add the correct single and double consonants from the box.

(a) ac_o_ _
(b) _u_ _y
(c) _e_ _ible
(d) to_o_ _ow
(e) in_e_ _upt
(f) di_a_ _ear
(g) pa_a_ _el
(h) be_i_ _ing
(i) ne_e_ _ary
(j) _u_ _est

rr	ll	r	r
ss	ss	f	g
rr	gg	t	c
nn	nn	m	s
rr		t	
pp		s	

REMEMBER

Always use a dictionary to check your spellings if you are unsure.

4 What pattern do you notice about vowels and consonants?

5 Use five of the words in sentences to show what they mean.

Extension >>>

6 Write out the words.
Add the correct double letters from the box.
There are two pairs of double letters in each word.
Check your spelling in a dictionary.

(a) su_ _ _ _d
(b) a_ _re_ _ive
(c) a_ _re_ _
(d) co_ _i_ _ee
(e) emba_ _a_ _
(f) po_ _e_ _

cc	ee
gg	ss
dd	ss
mm	tt
rr	ss
ss	ss

7 Use the words in sentences to show what they mean.

Feedback ↩

Single-syllable words ending in a consonant which is preceded by one vowel double their last letters when suffixes such as 'ing' or 'ed' are added.

However, many words containing double letters have more than one syllable and do not always stick to any rules. It is therefore important to consider strategies which help you remember the word.

Objective ·····>

- To identify patterns in pluralisation and construct rules for regular spellings.

Spelling Focus

- **Plural** means **more than one**. When we change something from **singular (one only)** to plural, the spelling often changes.

- The most common way of forming the plural of a noun is to add 's'.

  One green <u>bottle</u> standing on the wall
  Twenty green <u>bottles</u> standing on the wall

- When you form the plural of most nouns ending in 'ch', 'sh', 'ss' and 'x', you add 'es'.

  At the jumble sale I bought two bru<u>shes</u> in bo<u>xes</u>, some mat<u>ches</u> and three wine gla<u>sses</u>.

- There are exceptions to these rules.

  ox – oxen

Starter >

❶ Copy the sentences. After each noun write if it is singular (s) or plural (p). The first one is done for you.

ⓐ My mum goes to the shops every day.
  My mum (s) *goes to the shops* (p) *every day* (s).

ⓑ She buys vegetables and sweets for me.
ⓒ My friends were sitting on the benches in the park.
ⓓ They were talking about seeing foxes in the bushes by the church last night.
ⓔ All the churches in the area ring their bells regularly.
ⓕ The boys and girls were miserable.
ⓖ They had lost their bus passes.
ⓗ They will not be allowed on the buses any more.

❷ Explain how you know that the nouns with (p) after them are plurals.

Practice >>

3 Write out and complete these plurals:

ⓐ one bush + one bush = two _____
ⓑ one lunch + one lunch = two _____
ⓒ one smash + one smash = two _____
ⓓ one fox + one fox = two _____
ⓔ one kiss + one kiss = two _____
ⓕ one watch + one watch = two _____
ⓖ one glass + one glass = two _____
ⓗ one rash + one rash = two _____
ⓘ one ranch + one ranch = two _____

Check your answers in a dictionary.

> **REMEMBER**
>
> Changing singular nouns into the plural is easy when you know the rules. Most nouns follow the rules.

Extension >>>

4 Copy and complete the chart.
Find 10 nouns for each word ending.

s (or ss)	ch	sh	x
bus			
			ox

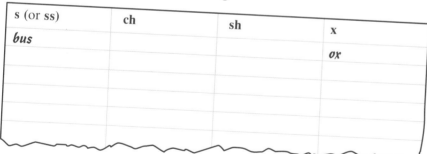

5 Write sentences using the words, first in the singular and then in the plural. Check your answers in a dictionary. (Be careful: some plurals may not follow these rules.)

> **Feedback** ↩
>
> In this unit you have practised and learned some rules associated with plurals – but there are others. For instance, consider nouns ending in 'y' and what happens to them when they are made plural. There are also nouns which do not change in the plural, for example, **sheep**.

Objective ·····>

- To consolidate spelling conventions concerning words using apostrophes.

Spelling Focus

- One use of **apostrophes** is to show omission (shortening words by leaving out letters).

  They are going to the concert. <u>We</u> <u>are</u> not.

  They're going to the concert. <u>We're</u> not.

- Apostrophes are also used to show possession (that something belongs to someone or something).

  My dog's collar (the collar of my dog)

  I have read Dickens's novels. (the novels of Dickens)

- People often confuse 'its' and 'it's'. It is important to learn the difference. 'It's' is a contraction. It means 'it is'. 'Its' is a possessive pronoun. It means 'belonging to'.

  Look at the alien. It's moving towards its spaceship.

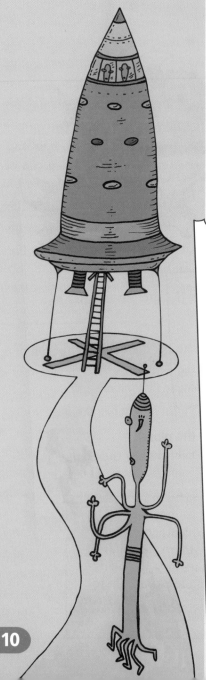

Starter >

1 Copy these sentences.
Change the words in bold to one word using an apostrophe.
Say which letters have been omitted.

(a) '**It is** a lovely day today,' Mrs Smith said.

(b) I am sure **they are** not going to come.

(c) '**It is** OK for you. **You are** never short of money,' he shouted.

(d) I think **it is** good to be able to play a musical instrument.

(e) If we live until **we are** one hundred, **we will** never win the lottery.

(f) **We are** never allowed out in the evening until **we have** finished our homework.

(g) **I will** make sure he never plays in the team again.

(h) My guitar teacher says **he is** the best in the country.

(i) I know **who is** behind the door.

(j) **Do not** feed the animals. **They will** bite!

Practice ≫

2 Copy these sentences, finding a shorter way to write the words in bold. Choose words from the box to help.

> *there, there's, their, theirs, they're*

(a) Please make sure **there is** coffee available at the meeting.
(b) Even if they shake hands **they are** never going to be friends.
(c) I never enjoy going **to that place**.
(d) We found **the property belonging to them**.
(e) Look at my car. It is difficult not to be envious of **the one they have**.
(f) Your hat is **over in that direction**.
(g) **There has** been no response to the advertisement.
(h) **The garden owned by them** is beautiful.
(i) **There is** no doubt about it. **They are** forged notes.
(j) Put **the money belonging to them**, **over in that place**.

Extension ≫≫

3 Rewrite these words putting the apostrophe in the correct place.

(a) Freds coat
(b) Kiplings stories
(c) The workmens hut
(d) Two girls coats
(e) A birds nest
(f) Charles spaniel
(g) A camels humps
(h) Two cats kittens
(i) An architects building

4 Punctuate the passage, putting in ten apostrophes.

'Im going to Julies party as a Roman,' said Max. 'Ive borrowed my mums sheets and it wont be hard to make a crown. Its easy to make one out of laurel leaves. Then Ill quote Shakespeare: 'Friends Romans Countrymen …'. These are Shakespeares most-quoted lines. Thatll make everyone know Ive been listening in class!'

REMEMBER

Singular words ending in 's' need an apostrophe + 's'. For example: King James's crown, the Princess's hat, Dickens's novels.

Feedback ↺

You have practised the spelling of contractions. This is when two words are shortened and made into one word, by leaving out some letters.

You have also practised the correct use of similar words, like 'it's' and 'its', and 'there' and 'they're'.

Objective ·····>

- To investigate the sounds of words and patterns of spelling.

Spelling Focus 📁

- Playing with words can make you see the differences in sound and the impact spelling can have on meaning.

  What did the fish say to his girlfriend?

  Come back to my plaice!

  Here *plaice* is a **homophone** of *place*. They sound the same but are spelled differently and mean something different.

- Playing with words can make you look more closely at them.

  Did you realise that 'star' is 'rats' backwards?

  Did you know that 'mug' is 'gum' backwards?

  These are known as **anagrams**.

Starter >

❶ Solve the anagrams.
Read the clues and write out the new words.
The first one is done for you.

ⓐ melon (a sour fruit) – *lemon*
ⓑ lime (a distance)
ⓒ sneak (a reptile)
ⓓ step (nuisance)
ⓔ wolves (not consonants)
ⓕ sword (what you write)
ⓖ plate (on a flower)
ⓗ cheap (a fruit)
ⓘ ocean (small boat)
ⓙ lamp (on your hand)

❷ Put the letters of these words in a different order to spell other words.
Make **two** anagrams for each word.
The first one is done for you.

ⓐ team – *meat, tame*
ⓑ flow
ⓒ tea
ⓓ evil
ⓔ peal
ⓕ slime
ⓖ stop
ⓗ time
ⓘ slate

Practice »

3 In an eighteenth century play, *The Rivals*, a character called Mrs Malaprop is always muddling her words. Write the correct version of these 'malapropisms'. Explain why the word originally chosen is incorrect. A dictionary may help.

(a) I am the most populous person in the school.
(b) The River Nile is essential to irritate the land.
(c) To speak properly you need to take electrocution lessons.
(d) She's a vivacious reader – she gets through ten books a week.
(e) When she heard the news she screamed and went into hydrostatics.

4 Use a dictionary to find the malapropisms from this passage from *The Rivals*. What did Mrs Malaprop really mean to say?

I would by no means wish a daughter of mine to be a progeny of learning ... she should have a supercilious knowledge in accounts; and, as she grew up, I would have her instructed in geometry, so that she might know something of the contagious countries. But above all Sir Anthony, she should be mistress of orthodoxy, so that she might not mis-spell, and mispronounce words so shamefully as girls usually do; and likewise that she might reprehend the true meaning of what she is saying.

Extension »»

5 Change one letter at a time to make new words in the chain. One example has been done for you.

him → *hem* → *her*

(a) warm _ _ _ _ card _ _ _ _ cold
(b) car _ _ _ bat _ _ _ bus
(c) boy _ _ _ _ _ _ lad
(d) well _ _ _ _ sill _ _ _ _ sick
(e) hard _ _ _ _ cart _ _ _ _ _ _ _ _ sort _ _ _ _
(f) rug _ _ _ _ _ _ bat
(g) west _ _ _ _ _ _ _ _ easy
(h) wet _ _ _ pat _ _ _ _ _ _ dry
(i) two _ _ _ _ _ _ _ _ _ _ _ _ fix
(j) cat _ _ _ _ _ _ dog
(k) new _ _ _ fed _ _ _ _ _ _ _ _ _ and _ _ _ odd

Feedback ↶

English as a language does not always follow logical sound patterns. It is important to listen to the sound of words and note exceptions that you find.

Unit 6: Prefixes

Objectives ····>

- To consolidate and secure spelling conventions.
- To build up spellings using known prefixes.

Spelling Focus

- A **prefix** is a **group of letters** that is added to the **beginning** of a word to change its meaning.

  happy can become <u>un</u>happy; way can become <u>sub</u>way

- Prefixes often come from Greek or Latin and can mean something quite specific.

- 'Pre' comes from Latin and means 'before'. So a 'prefix' is literally something that you 'fix' before the word.

- If you know the meaning of prefixes you will understand how words are built up of separate parts and how the spelling of a word has come about.

  Hence, you should now be able to understand the spelling of words such as: *<u>pre</u>pare, <u>pre</u>dict, <u>pre</u>historic*.

Starter >

❶ Write out the words and underline the prefixes. The first one is done for you.

  (a) *<u>un</u>happy, <u>un</u>like, <u>un</u>clear*
  (b) inside, inborn, incredible
  (c) surface, surname, surplus
  (d) prefix, prehistoric, precaution
  (e) exclaim, exit, extinguish
  (f) centipede, centurion, centimetre
  (g) dislike, disappear, disapprove
  (h) antidote, antibiotic, antifreeze
  (i) compound, compact, compare

❷ Look carefully at the meanings of the examples. Write what each prefix might mean. For example: a centipede has a hundred legs so 'cent' could mean 'one hundred'.

Practice »

3 Think of a word beginning with one of the prefixes in the Prefix Box to go with each meaning.

> **Prefix Box**
>
> *auto, bi, trans, tele, circum, tri, sub, mis*

(a) A vehicle with two wheels.
(b) The distance all around a circle.
(c) A person's handwritten signature.
(d) A boat which sails under water.
(e) Three children born at the same birth.
(f) Across the Atlantic Ocean.
(g) To choose wrongly.
(h) A device for reproducing sounds and for talking over a distance.

4 Find more examples of words which use each of these prefixes. Explain what they mean.

Extension »>

5 Copy and complete the chart. Use a dictionary to help.

Prefix	Meaning	Two examples
octo		octopus, octagon
semi		
mono		
anti		
quad		
re		
inter		
super		

Feedback ↩

Knowing the meaning of individual prefixes will enable you to understand other words containing the same prefix.

To find out more about prefixes and the derivation of words, you need an etymological dictionary – although any dictionary will contain a certain amount of information about derivation.

Objective •••••>

- To recognise and spell a range of suffixes that can be added to nouns and verbs to make adjectives.

Spelling Focus

- A **suffix** is a **group of letters** that we add to the **end** of a word. Suffixes may **change the purpose** of the word. Some nouns and verbs may be changed into adjectives by using different suffixes. For example, we can make the noun 'danger' into an adjective by adding the suffix 'ous'.

danger + ous = dangerous

It is dangerous to go any further.

We can make the verb 'wash' into an adjective by adding the suffix 'able'.

wash + able = washable

I'll have to wash your football kit. It's a good job it's washable.

Starter >

1 Add the suffix 'able' to these words to change them into adjectives.

Copy and complete the chart.

Original word	New adjective
crush	crushable
reason	
comfort	
suit	
credit	
favour	
remark	
fashion	

2 Does the spelling of the original root word change when you add the suffix 'able'?

Practice »

3 Write the root word of each of these adjectives.
Do it like this: *danger + ous = dangerous.*

(a) poisonous
(b) mountainous
(c) perilous
(d) villainous

4 Write the root word of each of these adjectives. Note that the
spelling of the root word might change slightly in some cases.

Do it like this: *famous – fame.*

(a) reliable
(b) victorious
(c) miserable
(d) envious
(e) impulsive
(f) childish

(g) studious
(h) energetic
(i) volcanic
(j) attractive
(k) foolish

Extension »»

5 Now write the adjectives from question 4 above in five distinct sets, according to their suffixes.

6 Copy these sentences. Fill in each gap with an adjective ending in 'ive', 'ous' or 'ic'. Look for clues in the sentences.

(a) Jim was a good athlete. He was very _ _ _ _ _ _ _ _.
(b) Tom knew how to express himself. His writing was very _ _ _ _ _ _ _ _ _ _.
(c) Emma was filled with envy. She was very _ _ _ _ _ _ _ _.
(d) I have never seen anyone so full of energy. James was really _ _ _ _ _ _ _ _ _.
(e) The fox continued to elude the hunters. It was very _ _ _ _ _ _ _ _.
(f) Ben liked to study. He was very _ _ _ _ _ _ _ _.
(g) How _ _ _ _ _ _ _ _ _ _! It was such a mystery!
(h) The giant was truly huge. He was _ _ _ _ _ _ _ _.

Feedback ↩

Adding a suffix changes the purpose, and sometimes the spelling, of the root word.

You need to identify any useful rules you can follow to spell these words correctly in the future.

Objective ·····>

- To recognise and spell words containing 'al' as a suffix and prefix.

Spelling Focus

- A **prefix** is a group of letters that we put **in front** of a word.
- A **suffix** is a group of letters that we add to the **end** of a word.
- Prefixes and suffixes **change the meaning** and **purpose** of a word.
- The letters 'al' may be used as both a prefix and a suffix.

  al + ways = always; music + al = musical

  I have always been musical.

- Notice that 'al' only ever has one 'l' when used as a prefix and a suffix.
- Notice that you create one word in each case.

  It may sound like two words (*all + ways*) but it is not.

Starter >

1 Add the prefix 'al' to these words.
Check your answers in a dictionary.

   (a) ways   (e) mighty
   (b) ready   (f) one
   (c) most   (g) though
   (d) so

2 Explain the difference between the following:

   (a) all ways; always
   (b) all mighty; almighty
   (c) all ready; already

Practice >>

3 Copy the sentences below. Choose an 'al' word to complete each one sensibly.

  (a) It was _ _ _ _ _ _ lunchtime before we finished.
  (b) When everyone left, I was _ _ _ _ _ .
  (c) I _ _ _ _ _ _ get up early in the summer.
  (d) When I got the latest trainers, my friend _ _ _ _ wanted some.
  (e) I tried hard, _ _ _ _ _ _ _ _ I knew the exam was difficult.

4 Change these nouns into adjectives. Copy and complete the chart.

Noun	Adjective
magic	magical
accident	
person	
comic	
coast	
season	
mechanic	

REMEMBER

'Al' is not written with a double 'l' – either at the beginning or the ending of a word.

Extension >>>

5 Find eight 'al' words in this wordsearch.
Say if the 'al' is used as a suffix or a prefix each time.

q	u	u	r	a	l	w	a	y	s	t	y	u	p
d	m	a	g	i	c	a	l	v	b	n	m	x	z
a	s	d	k	j	a	l	r	e	a	d	y	b	v
z	x	a	l	t	h	o	u	g	h	m	p	u	r
c	o	a	s	t	a	l	k	h	g	f	s	a	q
l	k	j	h	g	f	o	r	i	g	i	n	a	l
t	g	r	e	d	a	l	o	n	e	n	b	c	s
m	a	t	h	e	m	a	t	i	c	a	l	d	z

6 Write the root word of each of these 'al' words: *mechanical = mechanic*.
Note that the spelling of the root word may change slightly in some cases.

  (a) mathematical
  (b) tropical
  (c) universal
  (d) electrical
  (e) physical
  (f) theatrical
  (g) biblical
  (h) hysterical

Feedback

When you add 'al' as a prefix, notice that you create one word in each case. It may sound like two words but it is not. 'Always' has a different meaning from 'all ways'. The suffix 'al' can make adjectives, for example, *magical* or nouns like *arrival*.

Objective

- To recognise the way in which nouns and adjectives can be made into verbs by the use of suffixes.

Spelling Focus

- A **suffix** is a group of letters we add to the **end** of a word.
- **Suffixes** may **change the purpose** of a word.
- Some nouns or adjectives may be changed to verbs by using different suffixes. For example, we can add the suffix 'ise' to the adjective 'final' to make it into the verb 'to finalise'.

It is the <u>final</u> design. They will <u>finalise</u> the details of it.

We can add the suffix 'en' to the adjective 'sharp' to make it into the verb 'to sharpen'.

My pencil is not <u>sharp</u> so I will <u>sharpen</u> it.

Starter

❶ Make these adjectives into verbs by adding the suffix 'en'.
Copy and complete the chart.

Adjective	Verb
dark	darken
fast	
soft	
tight	
hard	
quick	
sweet	
short	
dead	

❷ Now make these adjectives into verbs.
Watch out for the spelling!

(a) fat   (c) sad
(b) loose   (d) wide

Practice >>

3 Write the 'ate' verb from which the following nouns come. Do it like this: *complication – to complicate*.

(a) operation
(b) punctuation
(c) communication
(d) celebration
(e) indication
(f) hesitation
(g) education
(h) termination

4 Write the root word from which each of these verbs is formed.
Do it like this: *to hospitalise – hospital*.
Note that the spelling of the root word may change slightly in some cases.

(a) categorise
(b) simplify
(c) magnetise
(d) purify
(e) equalise
(f) legalise
(g) nationalise
(h) signify
(i) glorify
(j) amplify
(k) characterise
(l) dramatise

Extension >>>

5 Choose the suffix 'ate', 'ise' or 'ify' to complete each word.
Use a dictionary if necessary.

(a) discrimin _ _ _
(b) horr _ _ _
(c) critic _ _ _
(d) superv _ _ _
(e) qual _ _ _
(f) associ _ _ _
(g) magn _ _ _
(h) econom _ _ _
(i) integr _ _ _

6 Using the words above, write some sentences so that the meaning is clear. Use a dictionary if necessary.

Feedback

When adding suffixes, it is useful to know the root word, as this will help you to understand if and why the spelling has to change.

You can also use spelling rules that you have learned elsewhere. For example, single-syllable words ending in a consonant which is preceded by one vowel double their last letter when suffixes such as 'en' are added.

fat ➤ *fatten*

Objective ·····>

* To spell regular verb endings 'ing' and 'ed'.

Spelling Focus

* We can change many verbs into the past tense by adding the suffixes 'ing' and 'ed'.

  Sheena was <u>zipping</u> up her coat. It was so cold she <u>zipped</u> it right up.

* With single-syllable verbs ending in one vowel and a consonant, we often have to double the final consonant before adding 'ing' or 'ed'.

  shop – shopping

* If verbs end in a consonant plus 'y' we just add 'ing'.

  cry – crying

  When we add 'ed' we have to change the 'y' to 'i' before adding 'ed'.

  The baby was <u>crying</u>. He <u>cried</u> until he was fed.

* If a verb ends in an 'e', we have to drop the 'e' before adding the suffix.

  hope – hoping

Starter >

❶ Copy and complete the chart.

Root verb	+ing	+ed
hop	hopping	
lag		lagged
pin		
hope		
hug		
pine		
bat		
dip		
love		
hum		

Practice »

2 Add 'ing' and 'ed' to each of these verbs.
Do it like this: *cry – crying – cried.*

(a) spy
(b) try
(c) rely
(d) deny

(e) apply
(f) reply
(g) occupy
(h) supply

(i) multiply
(j) dry

3 Write the root word of each of these verbs.
Do it like this: *cried – cry.*

(a) spied
(b) flying
(c) emptied
(d) copied

(e) defying
(f) terrifying
(g) buried
(h) occupied

(i) studying
(j) married

Extension »»

4 Copy the sentences below. Choose the correct form of the correct verb from the box to complete each sentence.

> *beg, carry, dim, fit, horrify, hurry,
> mop, multiply, rub, study*

(a) He _ _ _ _ _ _ _ to school because he was late.
(b) The poor man was _ _ _ _ _ _ _ in the street.
(c) The old lady was _ _ _ _ _ _ _ _ a black handbag.
(d) Alice _ _ _ _ _ _ _ hard for her exams.
(e) When the show began the lights _ _ _ _ _ _ .
(f) The cleaner _ _ _ _ _ _ the dirty floor.
(g) Mr Amin the carpenter _ _ _ _ _ _ some new cupboards in the classroom.
(h) Two _ _ _ _ _ _ _ _ _ _ by two equals four.
(i) Vicky was _ _ _ _ _ _ _ her sore head when her mother came in.
(j) Tom's dad was _ _ _ _ _ _ _ _ _ by the mess in the bedroom.

Feedback ↶

- Single-syllable verbs ending in a consonant preceded by one vowel double their last letters when suffixes such as 'ing' or 'ed' are added.
- If a verb ends in a consonant plus 'y' we just add 'ing': *cry – crying*. When we add 'ed' we have to change the 'y' to 'i' before adding 'ed': *cry – cried*.

Objective ·····⟩

- To recognise and spell the suffixes 'ary' and 'ic'.

Spelling Focus ▱

- A **suffix** is a group of letters we add to the **end** of a word.
- Suffixes change the **meaning or purpose** of the word.
- Adding 'ic' to a word generally makes it into an adjective – it describes a noun. For example:

  a gigantic dictionary

- When adding suffixes, it is useful to know the root word, as this will help you to understand if and why the spelling has to change. For example:

  realist (noun)

  realistic (adjective)

  moment (noun)

  momentary (adjective)

Starter ⟩

❶ Brainstorm as many words as you can that end with the suffix 'ic' or 'ary'.

Decide if they are nouns or adjectives.

❷ Copy the sentences below.
Use a suitable 'ic' word – an adjective – to complete each one.
Look for clues in each sentence.

- ⓐ An athlete is very _ _ _ _ _ _ _ _ .
- ⓑ Someone with a lot of energy is _ _ _ _ _ _ _ _ .
- ⓒ A giant is _ _ _ _ _ _ _ _ .
- ⓓ Something made of metal is _ _ _ _ _ _ _ _ .
- ⓔ Something that uses electricity is _ _ _ _ _ _ _ _ _ _ .
- ⓕ A volcano is _ _ _ _ _ _ _ _ .
- ⓖ An angel is _ _ _ _ _ _ _ .
- ⓗ A hero is _ _ _ _ _ _ .

Practice >>

3 Copy the words below. Use either 'ary' or 'ic' to complete each one. Use a dictionary if necessary.

(a) majest _____
(b) custom _____
(c) dynam _____
(d) poet _____

(e) moment _____
(f) necess _____
(g) elast _____
(h) realist _____

(i) milit _____
(j) artist _____
(k) automat _____
(l) station _____

4 Rewrite the words in two sets according to their 'ary' or 'ic' suffixes.

Extension >>>

5 These 'ary' and 'ic' words are all nouns. Each word has the wrong ending. Rewrite each word correctly. A dictionary will help. Copy and complete the chart.

Incorrect word	Correct word	Meaning
libric	library	
comary		
arithmetary		
dictionic		
secretic		
mechanary		
glossic		
magary		
critary		
tributic		

REMEMBER

Dealing with suffixes makes you more aware of how words are constructed.

6 Now complete the third column by finding the meanings of the words. A dictionary will help.

Feedback

You have learned how awareness of grammar and being able to recognise basic parts of speech, such as adjectives, can help you understand the spelling of some words.

Unit 12: Suffixes – 'ible'/'able'

Objective ·····›

- To recognise and spell the suffixes 'ible' and 'able'.

Spelling Focus 📄

- Two **common suffixes** are 'ible' and 'able'.

- It is often possible to see the whole root word when the suffix 'able' is added.

  comfort + able = comfortable

  fashion + able = fashionable

- It is often not possible to see the whole root word when the suffix 'ible' is added.

  terror + ible = terrible

  divide + ible = divisible

- There are always exceptions to spelling rules. Note examples and exceptions as you learn new words.

Starter ›

❶ Copy these words.
Circle the root words.
Are they complete or part root words?

- ⓐ reasonable
- ⓑ fashionable
- ⓒ remarkable
- ⓓ favourable
- ⓔ obtainable
- ⓕ considerable
- ⓖ punishable
- ⓗ laughable

❷ Divide the words into syllables to find the suffix.
Do it like this: *rea / son / able.*

Practice >>

3 Copy these words. Write the root word from which each comes. How do these words deviate from the rule set out in the Spelling Focus? The first one is done for you.

(a) believable – *believe*

(b) copiable

(c) excitable

(d) valuable

(e) reliable

4 Copy these words. Choose 'ible' or 'able' to complete each word. Use a dictionary if necessary.

(a) poss _ _ _ _

(b) horr _ _ _ _

(c) flex _ _ _ _

(d) suit _ _ _ _

(e) agree _ _ _ _

(f) sens _ _ _ _

(g) invis _ _ _ _

(h) incred _ _ _ _

(i) understand _ _ _ _

(j) cap _ _ _ _

(k) aud _ _ _ _

(l) divis _ _ _ _

Extension >>>

5 Copy all the words in the box.

> *manageable, knowledgeable, changeable, noticeable, serviceable, replaceable*

Write a sentence to say what you notice about the spelling of the root word after the suffix has been added.

6 Compare your findings in question 3 and question 5. Can you think of a reason why this difference should be? (Clue: what effect does the final 'e' have on the consonant before it? What happens if you remove this 'e' and add the suffix?)

7 Write five more 'able' and five more 'ible' words that have not been used anywhere in this unit.

Feedback

In this unit, you have explored the following spelling rule and identified exceptions to it.

It is often possible to see the whole root word when the suffix 'able' is added, for example:
favour + able = favourable

It is often not possible to see the whole root word when the suffix 'ible' is added, for example:
terror + ible = terrible

Objectives ····>

- To be aware of the usefulness of recognising suffixes.
- To distinguish between the sounds at the end of words.

Spelling Focus

- **Suffixes** are found at the **ends** of words. Both 'tion' and 'sion' are **common** suffixes.

- The suffixes 'tion' and 'sion' normally sound slightly different in words.

  vision ('sion' usually sounds like '**zhun**')

  attention ('tion' sounds like '**shun**')

  However, there are exceptions.

- This unit will identify ways to help you use the correct suffix at the end of words.

Starter >

1 Add 'tion' or 'sion' to these words.
Write the words. Check in a dictionary.

- (a) na
- (b) revi
- (c) sta
- (d) confu   + tion?
- (e) opera   + sion?
- (f) divi
- (g) invita
- (h) educa
- (i) deci

REMEMBER

A 'shun' sound is mostly spelled with 'tion' as in 'action' – but look out for 'mansion', 'cushion', 'ocean', 'musician' or 'suspicion'.

Practice »

❷ Write the correct noun made from the verb in brackets. Underline the suffixes. Do it like this: *to televise – the televi<u>sion</u>.*

Check your spelling in a dictionary.

ⓐ My dad told me to turn off the (to televise).
ⓑ There was much (to confuse) after the bomb.
ⓒ He was pleased at his (to include) in the football team.
ⓓ The soil had been worn away by (to erode).
ⓔ He heard the enormous (to explode) several miles away.
ⓕ She had not done much (to revise) for her exam.
ⓖ His (to decide) to leave the team was regrettable.
ⓗ The class was sad to hear about her (to exclude) from the school.

❸ Find three more examples of verbs that can be changed into nouns using this ending. Explain what changes happen to the verb.

Extension »»

❹ Copy and complete the chart.
Underline the common letter string in the words

Verb	Noun	Changes in spelling
to operate	an operat<u>ion</u>	Drop the final 'e'. Add 'ion'.
to invent		
to create		
to celebrate		
to relate		
to add		
to introduce		

REMEMBER

The suffixes 'sion' and 'tion' can sound different, but can also sound the same (e.g. ascension, conversion).

❺ Add three more examples of your own to the chart.

Feedback ↩

Suffixes are very important in spelling.

If you realise that words are made up of parts, and common suffixes are one of these parts, then you can put words together more easily.

Through your investigations you have also realised the importance of correctly sounding out these suffixes.

Objectives ····>

- To learn to spell polysyllabic words containing unstressed vowels.
- To sound out and syllabify words.

Spelling Focus

- A **polysyllabic** word is a word with **more than one syllable**.

- Sometimes, some vowels in these words are not always 'stressed' or pronounced directly. For example, in the words below, the 'e' sounds are often missed out or hardly noticeable.

diff<u>e</u>rent

int<u>e</u>rest

- Words containing unstressed vowels are some of the most commonly misspelled words. This unit will look at a number of strategies for avoiding problems.

– One strategy is to break the word into syllables.

sep /ar / ate

Starter >

❶ Write out these words, filling each gap with a vowel. Use a dictionary to help.

(a) alc _ h _ l
(b) b _ ch _ lor
(c) b _ s _ ness
(d) cal _ nd _ r
(e) cem _ t _ ry

(f) col _ n _ l
(g) fore _ gn
(h) g _ ar _ nt _ e
(i) secr _ t _ ry
(j) sep _ r _ te

Practice >>

2 These eight words have been broken into their separate syllables.
Choose a syllable from each column as required.
Join the syllables and write the words.

(a) pois   ter   ful   –
(b) ter   per   ent   ure
(c) in   on   est   –
(d) beau   pa   at   –
(e) dif   rif   ous   ing
(f) com   ta   ble   –
(g) tem   ti   ic   –
(h) por   fer   ny   –

REMEMBER

Sound out the words. Make sure you stress any vowels when you are conscious of them.

3 Circle the vowel in each word which is unstressed when spoken aloud.

Extension >>>

4 Look at the words in the box.

extraterritorial, signature, celebration, temperature, independent, description, stationary, freedom, different

Now copy and complete the chart.
Knowing about the structure and derivation of words can help you spot where vowels in polysyllabic words should go.

Root word	Any prefix	Any suffix
territory	extra	ial

Feedback

You have investigated two strategies for spelling polysyllabic words.

- Break the words into syllables, sounding out each part and recognising the rhythm of the words.

- Consider the derivation of parts of the words. In this way, you will once again break the words into their separate parts.

Objective ·····>

- To identify word roots, derivations and spelling patterns.

Spelling Focus

- A **word root** is a basic word to which a **prefix** and/or a **suffix** can be added to make a different word.

  'Clear' is a word by itself.

  It is the root of *'unclear'* and *'clearly'*.

- Recognising root words enables you to see how prefixes and suffixes add to the meaning of a word.

  For example:

  'hypo' comes from Greek for *'under'*

  'dermis' comes from Greek for *'skin'*

  'hypodermic' is a needle put *'under the skin'*.

- Use an etymological dictionary where possible.

Starter >

1 Write out the words and underline the word roots in each example.

Write by the side of each word whether a prefix or a suffix has been used to change the word root.

The first one has been done for you.

(a) *helping (suffix), unhelpful (prefix and suffix), helpless (suffix)*

(b) malformation, conformity, reform

(c) childhood, childish, children

(d) invent, prevent, advent

(e) impart, apart, departure

(f) pressure, pressing, depress

(g) microphone, telephone, phonics

(h) signal, signature, signed

Practice ≫

2 Look at the words in the box below.

> ordinary, terrestrial, scope, copy, marine, approve, appear, way, graph, wave, market, social

Make some new words by adding a suffix or a prefix from the boxes below. For example:

ordinary – <u>extra</u>ordinary; copy – copy<u>ing</u>

Use a dictionary to check your words.

> **Prefixes**
> dis, extra, sub, micro, photo, super, anti

> **Suffixes**
> ing, ed, ic, ing, al

3 Write the words in sentences to show that you understand them.

Extension ≫≫

4 Many word roots come from ancient languages such as Latin and are not whole words. Some examples are shown below.

> *dico, dictus* (I say, said); *scribo, scriptus* (I write, written); *voco, vocatus* (I call, called); *audio, auditus* (I hear, heard); *pes, pedis* (the foot, of the foot); *sonus* (a sound); *terra* (earth); *novus, nova* (new).

Copy and complete the chart.
Find words which use these ancient word roots.

Ancient word root	Meaning	Examples
dico, dictus	I say, said	dictation, dictionary

Feedback ↩

Understanding the derivation of root words enables us to spell other related words more easily. To find out more about the derivation of words you will need an etymological dictionary, although any dictionary will contain some useful information.

Unit 16: Mnemonics

Objective ·····>

- To invent and use mnemonics for irregular or difficult spellings.

Spelling Focus

- **Mnemonics** are ways we invent to **help us remember** something.

- Words can be divided into syllables that tell us what parts of the words mean.

  The suffix *'ology'* is Greek for the 'study of' - astrology is the study of the stars and can be used to tell fortunes.

- We can make up rules to tell us how to spell particular letter strings: *'i' before 'e' except after 'c'*.

- **Acronym** (a word made from the initial letters of a series of words) can help to remember shorter words.

  Wasps Always Sting = WAS

- Inventing short stories or phrases can help us remember spellings.

  Every morning the *MAN GOES* to his garden and picks *MANGOES* for his breakfast.

- Finding smaller words hidden in the longer word can help.

  Colin ATE all the chocolATE.

Starter >

1 The following are subjects that can be studied.
Use a dictionary to find the meaning of each.
Invent mnemonics to complete the chart.
The first one is done for you.

Subject	Meaning	Mnemonic
Astrology	The study of the star's, planets and moon to understand human behaviour.	'astr' is an anagram of 'star'
Biology		
Psychology		
Sociology		
Technology		
Archaeology		

Practice >>

2 Write mnemonics for each of the following words.

k	g	e	p	g
n	n	x	l	h
i	o	c	e	o
f	m	i	n	s
e	e	t	t	t
		i	e	
		n	o	
		g	u	
			s	

REMEMBER

Everyone learns words in a different way. What works for you is what matters.

3 For each word, write a paragraph of a story to help you remember the spellings.

Extension >>>

4 How many smaller words can you find in each of the following.

(a) misshapen
(b) rebellion
(c) valedictory
(d) loathsome
(e) pendant
(g) superintendent

5 Find 5 more words that can be divided into smaller words. Use a dictionary to help you.

Feedback ↻

Mnemonics are personal to you. They may appear 'silly' but if they help you then the strategy has worked!

Think about which of these you really find useful when spelling difficult words:

- The sound of a word?
- The pattern a word makes?
- Making up a rhyme or a mnemonic?

Objective ·····>

- To build words from other known words, from the meaning and derivation of words.

Spelling Focus

- It is possible to build up longer words from smaller words or parts of words.

- If you know the spelling and the meaning of one word it can help you to spell a variety of words.

  For example, if you can spell **press**, then you can spell **de_press_, ex_press_, im_press_, sup_press_** and **re_press_** just by adding prefixes.

  If you can spell **sign**, then you can spell **_sign_al, _sign_ificant** and **_sign_ature** by adding suffixes.

- If you know the derivation of words it can help.

  For example, **'dis'** or **'mis'** at the beginning of a word can make it mean the opposite.

  approve – disapprove

Starter >

1 Copy the examples.
   Underline the word or part of a word which appears in each.
   The first one is done for you.

   (a) _shape_less, mis_shap_en, re_shaped_
   (b) telephone, telescopic, television
   (c) xylophone, microphone, headphone
   (d) advent, invention, preventing
   (e) reigning, sovereign, foreign
   (f) disgraceful, graced, gracious
   (g) appearance, disappear, appeared

2 Use your dictionary to find out what the underlined sections mean.

Practice >>

3 You can build compound words from known words.
For example: *play + ground = playground, play + house = playhouse, play + thing = plaything.*
List at least two compound words built using each of the following words.

(a) silver   (d) water   (g) ear   (j) red
(b) hair   (e) stock   (h) sun   (k) snow
(c) some   (f) honey   (i) foot   (l) counter

4 Use your dictionary to find out what these new words mean and to check your spelling.

Extension >>>

5 Add prefixes and suffixes to each root word to make as many new words as possible.
For example, with 'approve' you could make: *approves, approving, approved, approval, disapproval* and so on.

Root words	Prefixes	Suffixes
approve	dis	ing
continue	un	ed
assume	in	ance
crease	de	al
direct	mis	s
part	im	ure
place	re	ment

Feedback ↻

- You have learned how words are built up from 'parts' of words you know already, e.g. root words, prefixes and suffixes.
- You can spell longer words by sounding them out and building them up as you write them.
- You can find ways of spelling words by identifying and recognising the smaller parts within the words.

Unit 18: Compound words

Objective •••••➤

- To build up spellings by syllabic parts.

Spelling Focus 📁

- **Compound** words are words made up by **joining** together **complete words**.

  any + one = anyone; black + berry = blackberry.

- All long words can be broken down into **smaller parts** called **syllables**.

  Bad has one syllable.

  Bad / min / ton has three syllables.

- Each syllable must contain a vowel sound. Remember that a 'y' often acts as a vowel.

- Syllables do not have to make whole words by themselves.

- You can make new words from separate syllables.

Starter ➤

❶ Match up each word from Column A with a word from Column B to make compound words. Write the new words.

Column A	Column B
foot	ache
snow	ball
head	band
play	bow
post	box
night	day
rain	ground
farm	man
birth	mare
head	yard

❷ Write five more compound words of your own.

Practice »

3 Join up one syllable from each column to make complete words.
Write out the words like this: **al/to/geth/er**.

a al	er	dar	–
b cal	per	ar	le
c ex	to	ab	y
d gov	u	geth	ure
e tem	ess	ar	–
f val	u	ment	tion
g ed	ru	ar	–
h dic	tion	at	y
i nec	en	ca	er
j Feb	ern	cise	y

> **REMEMBER**
>
> Every syllable needs a vowel (or vowel sound such as a 'y').

Extension »»

4 Write out the words on the Ancient Rome Word List.
Add the correct vowels. Check the spellings and meanings of the words in a dictionary or a history book if you are unsure.

Ancient Rome Word List

a cl _ ss _ c _ l	**h** r _ p _ bl _ c _ n	**o** _ q _ _ d _ ct
b P _ mp _ _ _	**i** C _ _ s _ r	**p** c _ r _ m _ ny
c v _ ll _	**j** m _ l _ t _ ry	**q** ch _ r _ _ t
d _ tr _ _ m	**k** c _ nt _ r _ _ n	**r** _ rb _ n
e gl _ d _ _ t _ r	**l** _ mp _ r _ r	**s** t _ mpl _
f s _ n _ t _ r	**m** c _ rc _ s	**t** sl _ v _ ry
g t _ g _	**n** l _ g _ _ n _ ry	

5 Count up the syllables in each word, e.g. **Ro/man** (2).

Feedback ↩

Compound words are formed by joining two shorter words together into one long word. This gives you insight into how some words are constructed.

Breaking words into their syllables is also helpful in spelling. Each syllable is like a beat in a word. Say words slowly and hear where breaks occur. Sound out each part of the word and note how the word is constructed in terms of vowels and consonants.

Unit 19: Letter strings

- To develop spelling strategies.
- To build up spellings using known letter strings.

Spelling Focus

- A **letter string** is a **group of letters** which **occurs frequently** in words. Letter strings help us to spell. For example:

  'tion' is a letter string in:
  attention
  perfec<u>tion</u>
  men<u>tion</u>ed.

- The letter 'q' is always followed by 'u' in English. The 'qu' letter string is found in words such as:

  q<u>u</u>ite
  req<u>u</u>est
  uniq<u>u</u>e
  soliloq<u>u</u>y.

- You can see that being aware of letter strings is very important in spelling.

Starter >

❶ Copy the words.
Underline the letter strings 'qu' and 'tion' that you find in them. The first one is done for you.

(a) **sq<u>u</u>adron**   squashed   **mosq<u>u</u>itoes**
(b) attention   section   sequestration
(c) quite   quiet   frequently
(d) conversation   organisation   sensation
(e) situation   population   nations
(f) request   liquorice   quarrel
(g) mentioned   reception   relations
(h) quiz   quiver   squint

40

Practice »

2 Copy and complete these words, using the letter string 'tion'.

(a) func
(b) competi
(c) circula — + tion
(d) prescrip
(e) frac

(f) perfec
(g) exclama
(h) informa — + tion
(i) junc
(j) indiges

3 Change these verbs into nouns. Do it like this:
to direct – the direction

(a) to create
(b) to add
(c) to subtract
(d) to prepare
(e) to compare

Write the nouns and verbs in sentences.
Use a dictionary to help you.

Extension »»

4 Solve the puzzles. All the answers contain 'qu'.

(a) Wife of a king
(b) A tank for fish
(c) Some old, valuable objects
(d) Large tent
(e) Feather cover for bed
(f) Use this instead of cash to pay someone
(g) Only one of its kind
(h) Small animal with bushy tail
(i) A line of people
(j) A fancy dress ball where you cover your face

5 Copy the chart.

Write the answers from the puzzle into the correct columns.

'qu' at the beginning	'qu' in the middle	'qu' at the end

REMEMBER

If 'qu' is the last sound in a word it is followed by a silent 'e', e.g. cheque, mosque.

Feedback ↩

Spelling is made easier by knowing some rules. For example, 'q' is always followed by 'u' in English.

Objective ·····>

- To investigate words which have common letter strings but different pronunciation.

Spelling Focus

- A **letter string** is a **group of letters** which frequently occurs in words.

- Remembering letter strings can help us to spell, but sometimes the same letter string can be pronounced in many different ways:

  'tough' sounds like *'stuff'*

  'although' sounds like *'oh'*

  'plough' sounds like *'now'*

  'thought' sounds like *'or'*.

- If you realise that words are made up of parts, and common letter strings are one of these parts, then you can put words together more easily, because you can identify the parts of words.

Starter >

1 Copy the chart.
Underline the common letter string in each row across.
The first one is done for you.

brown	frown	growl	show
rough	tough	plough	enough
moon	blood	tool	boot
course	flour	sour	hourly
pain	Spain	raining	said
heating	bear	treatment	seat
floating	coat	roar	moat

2 Circle the word with a different pronunciation in each row.

Practice ≫

3 Look at the pairs of words below. They have common letter strings but are pronounced differently and mean something different.
The first one is done for you.

(a) *bow (for firing arrows)*   *bow (bend down low)*

(b) sow   sow

(c) row   row

(d) wind   wind

(e) lead   lead

Use a dictionary and write sentences showing their different meanings.
The first one has clues to start you off.

Extension ≫≫

4 Consider the words in the box.

> *bought, through, tough, thought, ought, thorough, enough, trough, bough, nought, drought, although, though, hiccough*

Copy and complete the chart. Choose 'ough' words from the box above which are pronounced the same way as these five words.
Write them underneath the same-sounding words.

fought	rough	dough	plough	cough

5 Which words do not fit into any of the columns?

6 Write five sentences using one 'ough' word from each column.

Feedback ↶

It is important to be able to identify letter strings. This will help you with spelling. However, some letter strings can make different sounds, so it is difficult to make rules. Therefore it is sometimes better to group words by the sounds they have in common.

Unit 21: Silent letters

Objective ·····>

- To apply spelling rules and recognise exceptions.

Spelling Focus

- Some words are difficult to spell because they contain letters which are not pronounced – they are 'silent'.

  A __knight__ is on his __knees__.

  Centuries ago, people used to pronounce the 'k' in these words but over time this pronunciation was dropped.

- Other silent letters such as *'p'* in *'receipt'* were added by sixteenth century printers to make words look more like Latin.

- Silent letters in English are a historical curiosity. Very often the letters used to be pronounced, but as English has changed over the centuries such letters are no longer pronounced.

Starter >

❶ Write out these tongue twisters, inserting the silent letters.

    ⓐ A _night with _nobbly _nees once _new how to _nit while _neeling with a _napsack on his back.

    ⓑ The plum_er's thum_ became num_ as he clim_ed.

    ⓒ _nomes and _nats like to _nash and _naw.

    ⓓ G_ostly g_ouls eat g_oulish g_erkins.

    ⓔ The _riter was _retched after _renching his _ristwatch and _recking it.

❷ Write your own tongue twisters using the silent letter 'l' in words such as 'chalk' and 'folk'.

Practice >>

3 Identify the words which have silent letters and add them to the chart.

queen, knot, plumber, wheel, wash, knee, lamb, wreck, climb, gnat, debt, raspberry, island, rhyme, science, wrestle, hymn, knife, chemist, thumb, listen, rabbit, write, rough, autumn, sign, gnome, ghost, whistle, honour, vehicle, should, salmon, fasten, stalk, crumb, jump, wriggle, rhyme, pneumatic

Silent letter at beginning of word	Silent letter in middle of word	Silent letter at end of the word

4 Add six more words containing silent letters to the chart.

5 Say which letters come before or after the silent letters to make them 'silent'.

Extension >>>

6 Copy and complete the chart to write rules which will help you spell words with silent letters.

Silent letter	Rule	Two examples
	Comes after 'm' at the end of a syllable or a word. Also before 't'.	climb, debt
	Silent after 's'.	
	Comes before 'n'.	
	Follows 'w' and 'r'. Also found at the start of words.	
	Silent before 's', 'n' or 't'.	
	Sometimes silent in front of 'h'.	
	Silent after 'm'.	
	Sometimes silent in front of 'd', 'k' and 'm'.	

Feedback ↩

This unit has shown you that silent letters mostly follow a set of rules. Once the words are investigated and the rules established, you should find the spelling of these words easy.

Objective ·····>

- To identify words which have been borrowed from other languages.

Spelling Focus

- The English language is always changing.

- Each time England was invaded, many hundreds of years ago – by the Anglo-Saxons, by the Vikings, by the French – a new language was introduced and new words were added.

  For example: *skirt, village, knife*

- New words continued to be added in the nineteenth century through our connection with India and places further afield than Europe.

  For example: *verandah, curry, thug*

- Words are still being added today, for example from America and through films and music.

  For example: *rap, movie*

Starter >

1 Copy these words to do with food and eating.
Using a dictionary, write what they mean and from which country they are derived.

ⓐ dessert ⓓ chef
ⓑ buffet ⓔ menu
ⓒ café ⓕ hors d'oeuvre

2 Match the foods with the country from which they are derived.
Use your dictionary.

Foods	Country
pizza	Greece
cookies	Mexico
samosa	Italy
moussaka	USA
chocolate	India

Practice >>

3 Copy the chart below. Use your dictionary and other reference sources to sort these words and abbreviations into the correct columns.

mosque, supermarket, piano, p.m., fiancée, caravan, gangster, soprano, a.m., au pair, sherbet, teenager, opera, A.D., ballet, alcohol, detergent, fiasco, per annum, garage, mattress, powwow, spaghetti, centurion, lieutenant

From Arabic	From Latin	From American	From French	From Italian

4 Find another word to write in each of the columns.

Extension >>>

5 Find out in which countries these sports originated.
- (a) polo
- (b) tobogganing
- (c) skiing
- (d) baseball
- (e) judo
- (f) karate

6 Find out from which countries these words have been borrowed.
- (a) buoy
- (b) cot
- (c) khaki
- (d) sugar
- (e) tomato
- (f) bungalow
- (g) moccasin
- (h) tobacco
- (i) waltz
- (j) pyjamas
- (k) yacht
- (l) yoghurt

Write the meanings of any words you do not know.

7 Use five of the words in sentences to show you understand what they mean.

Feedback

Understanding root words can help you with remembering how to spell words and to appreciate where words originate. Many root words come from Latin or Greek, or other languages.

Study the etymology of words. A good dictionary will tell you the origins of words. You need to be able to identify the roots of words and also be able to see what happens when we add a prefix or a suffix – or both – to the root word.

Objective •••••>

- To understand how words and expressions have changed over time.

Spelling Focus

- Our language is always changing. Some words remain from centuries ago, but some have disappeared or their meaning has changed.

- We no longer use words such as *'thou'* – we use *'you'*; *'nice'* used to mean *'fussy'* or *'precise'*.

- We no longer use Shakespearean words such as *'visage'* meaning *'face'* or *'rude'* meaning *'rough'*.

- Language changes over time and words sometimes change their meaning. However, we can still understand much of what Chaucer wrote.

You can find information about the history and derivation of words in an etymological dictionary.

Starter >

❶ Copy and complete the chart to show how words to do with cinema and music have changed meaning.

Use a dictionary.

Word	Used to only mean	Today's extra meaning
shot	Shot from a gun	A photograph
rock	A rock on the ground	
still	Not moving	
album	A thing to put photographs in	
film	A thin covering	
band	A strip to hold together	
pop	A loud sound	
location	A special place	

Practice >>

2 These words have all changed their meaning over time.
Use a dictionary to link them to their old meaning.
Write what they mean today.

(a) awful   a peasant
(b) terrific   fussy
(c) horrid   food
(d) villain   worth nothing
(e) nice   causing terror
(f) meat   rough, bristly
(g) naughty   full of wonder

3 Write sentences using five of the words to show what they mean today.

Extension >>>

4 Here is a passage from a poem written in 1390, describing a man who looked after a knight.

Write it in modern English.

> Of twenty yeer of age he was, I gesse.
> Of his stature he was of evene length,
> And wonderly delyvere and of great strengthe …
> Syngynge he was or floytynge al the day;
> He was as fressh as is the month of May.
> Short was his gowne, with sleves long and wyde.
> Wel koude he sitte on hor and fair ryde.

(from The Squire's Tale by Geoffrey Chaucer)

stature – height,   *delyvere* – lively,
floytynge – playing the flute,   *gowne* – outfit

5 Which words can you recognise?
Which words have changed?

Feedback ↩

Looking at the derivation of words can show us how words are made up of smaller parts – words within words – or can give us clues and understanding about how words developed.

49

Objective ·····>

- To distinguish between homophones.

Spelling Focus

- The following three words **sound** the **same**, have **different meanings** and are **spelled differently**. They are called **homophones**.

The <u>poor</u> dog has hurt its <u>paw</u>. <u>Pour</u> it a drink of water.

The English language has many homophones. They can only be distinguished when placed in a particular context or when we see them written down. In order to spell them correctly you need to associate a spelling with a context.

'Their' is for possession; *'they're'* contains a pronoun and a verb.

If you were in a church you would see an *'altar'*; *'alter'* means *'to change'*.

Starter >

1 Copy these sentences.
Underline the homophones.
The first one is done for you.

  (a) *He <u>ate</u> dinner every day at <u>eight</u>.*
  (b) The saw cut his hand and his fingers felt sore all week.
  (c) In the film the criminals tried to steal the money from the steel strongroom.
  (d) A hare is like a rabbit but with shorter hair.
  (e) Lewis Carroll wrote a tale about a mouse with a very long tail.
  (f) The naval commander bought a new sail for the ship at the dockyard sale.
  (g) She drew a flower shape in the spilt flour in the kitchen.
  (h) What do you call a bear in the shower? A bare bear!

2 Use a dictionary to find out what the homophones mean.

Practice >>

3 Match up the homophones from the box.
Write them out in pairs.

> fur, course, stair, fir, allowed, read, write, stare, reed, coarse, aloud, right

4 Copy the sentences.
Choose the correct homophone from the box to fill the gap.

(a) Many people think it is cruel to make _____ coats.
(b) To _____ at someone is considered rude.
(c) He was not _____ to go to the concert.
(d) This is not the _____ answer.
(e) I learned to _____ books when I was five.
(f) The material of the jacket felt very _____.

Extension >>>

5 Copy the chart.
Match the homophones.
Find a third homophone to go with each pair. Use a dictionary to help you. The first one is done for you.

poor	paw	pour
two	they're	
pear	fore	
there	reign	
rain	to	
rode	pare	
four	road	

6 Write sentences using these homophones.

Feedback ↻

Homophones are words that sound the same but have different meanings and spellings. Make a note of examples when you come across them. Think of mnemonics or other strategies that will help you to distinguish between homophones and help you to spell them.

Unit 25: Common spelling errors

Objective ·····>

- To learn complex polysyllabic words and unfamiliar words which do not conform to regular patterns.

Spelling Focus 📁

- Many words seem difficult to spell because no rules seem to apply to them.
- This unit will highlight a variety of ways to help you to spell and understand difficult words. These include:
  - looking for prefixes and word roots that will help you to investigate the derivation of the word
  - breaking the words into syllables and pronouncing each part
  - identifying smaller words in larger words
  - inventing mnemonics from the words
  - using the Look, Say, Cover, Write, Check spelling strategy.

  You don't need to use all these methods every time, but it is useful to have them available when you face a problem.

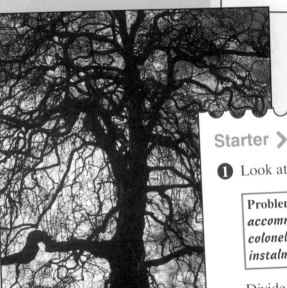

Starter >

1 Look at the commonly misspelled words in the Problem Box.

> **Problem Box**
> accommodation, acknowledge, aerial, annihilate, caricature, colonel, conscious, secretary, descendant, guarantee, instalment, occasion, recommend, surprise

Divide the words into syllables and pronounce each part. Copy and complete the chart. Rewrite each word using the Look, Say, Cover, Write, Check spelling strategy.

Word	Syllables				
	1st	2nd	3rd	4th	5th
accommodation	ac	com	mo	da	tion
acknowledge					
aerial					

Practice »

2 Look for small words in these larger words below.

> separate, altogether, apartment, awkward, bachelor, bankruptcy, business, calendar, cemetery, criticism, environment, foreigner, gases, gauge, opportunity, possession, privilege

Copy and complete the chart. Rewrite each word using the Look, Say, Cover, Write, Check spelling strategy.

Word	Smaller words I have found
separate	par, rate

REMEMBER

Everyone learns to spell words in a different way. What works for you is what matters.

3 Make mnemonics from the words you find.
For example: *SePARate is PAR for the course*.

Extension »»

4 Consider the words in the box below. Look for prefixes, suffixes or roots which will help you with the derivation of the words in the box. Use a dictionary to help. An etymological dictionary will be even better.

> beautiful, fluorescent, liaison, prejudice, rhyme, silhouette, vehicle, amateur, camouflage, descendant, exercise, calibre

Copy and complete the chart. Rewrite each word using the Look, Say, Cover, Write, Check spelling strategy.

Word	Derivation	Other words I have found that use the same prefix, suffix or root
beautiful	beau – French	

5 Find other words that use the same prefix, suffix or root as the words above.

Feedback ↻

Which of these do *you* find most useful when spelling difficult words:

- The sound and pattern of a word?
- Making up a rhyme or a mnemonic?
- Breaking words up into parts?
- Knowing the derivation of a word?

Objective ·····>

- To secure the spelling of key terms and new words from across the curriculum.

Spelling Focus

- Many words in History are specific to the period being studied. However there are words useful to anyone studying the subject.

This unit will highlight a variety of ways to help you to spell and understand these words. These include:

– looking for prefixes and word roots that will help you to investigate the derivation of the word

– breaking the words into syllables and pronouncing each part

– identifying smaller words in larger words

– inventing mnemonics from the words

– using the Look, Say, Cover, Write, Check spelling strategy.

You don't need to use all these methods every time, but it is useful to have them available when you face a problem.

Starter >

1 Look at the commonly misspelled words in the Problem Box.

> **Problem Box**
> bias, agricultural, citizen, colony, document, economical, invasion, politics, rebellion, religious, traitor, motivation, conflict

Divide the words into syllables and pronounce each part. Copy and complete the chart. Rewrite each word using the Look, Say, Cover, Write, Check spelling strategy.

Word	Syllables				
	1st	2nd	3rd	4th	5th
bias	bi	as			
agricultural					
citizen					

Practice »

2 Look for small words in the larger words below.

> government, Catholic, constitution, dynasty, defence, disease, emigration, priest, Protestant, revolution, independence

REMEMBER

Everyone learns words in a different way.

Copy and complete the chart. Rewrite each word using the Look, Say, Cover, Write, Check spelling strategy.

Word	Smaller words I have found
government	govern

3 Make mnemonics from the words you find.
For example: *GOVERNment GOVERNs*.

Extension »»

4 Consider the words in the box below. Look for prefixes, suffixes or roots which will help you with the derivation of the words. Use a dictionary to help. An etymological dictionary will be even better.

> cathedral, chronology, civilisation, imperialism, contradiction, parliament, propaganda, republic, medieval, democracy

Copy and complete the chart. Rewrite each word using the Look, Say, Cover, Write, Check spelling strategy.

Word	Derivation	Other words I have found that use the same prefix, suffix or root
cathedral	cathedra – Latin meaning 'seat'	

5 Find other words that use the same prefix, suffix or root as the words above.

Feedback ↻

Think about which of these help *you* most.

- The sound or the pattern of a word?
- Making up a rhyme or a mnemonic?
- Breaking words up into their constituent parts or identifying smaller words inside them?
- Knowing the derivation of a word?

Unit 27: ICT words

Objective ·····>

- To secure the spelling of key terms and new words from across the curriculum.

Spelling Focus

- Many words to do with ICT are new. Some words, such as **gigabyte**, have been created to describe something recently invented. Some words, such as 'mouse', have taken on new meanings.

- This unit will highlight a variety of ways to help you to spell and understand ICT words. These include:

  – looking for prefixes and word roots that will help you to investigate the derivation of the word

  – breaking the words into syllables and pronouncing each part

  – identifying smaller words in larger words

  – inventing mnemonics from the words

  – using the Look, Say, Cover, Write, Check spelling strategy.

  You don't need to use all these methods every time, but it is useful to have them available when you face a problem.

Starter >

1 Look at the commonly misspelled words in the Problem Box.

> **Problem Box**
> *cable, connection, document, input, Internet, memory, modem, processor, program, scanner, server, preview, output*

Divide the words into syllables and pronounce each part. Copy and complete the chart. Rewrite each word using the Look, Say, Cover, Write, Check spelling strategy.

Word	Syllables				
	1st	2nd	3rd	4th	5th
cable	ca	ble			
connection					
document					

Practice >>

2 Look for small words in the larger words below.

> keyboard, computer, delete, hardware, software, justify, megabyte, module, network, motherboard, password, spreadsheet

Copy and complete the chart. Rewrite each word using the Look, Say, Cover, Write, Check spelling strategy.

REMEMBER

Everyone learns subject specific words in a different way.

Word	Smaller words I have found
keyboard	key, board, oar, boar

3 Make mnemonics from the words you find.
For example: You KEY with a KEYboard.

Extension >>>

4 Consider the words in the box below. Look for prefixes, suffixes or roots which will help you with the derivation of the words. Use a dictionary to help. An etymological dictionary will be even better.

> binary, cartridge, cursor, database, electronic, graphic, digital, icon, interactive, interface, monitor, multimedia, sensor, virus

Copy and complete the chart. Rewrite each word using the Look, Say, Cover, Write, Check spelling strategy.

Word	Derivation	Other words I have found that use the same prefix, suffix or root
binary	'bi' means 'two'	

5 Find other words that use the same prefix, suffix or root as the words above.

Feedback ↻

Think about which of these help *you* most:

- The sound or the pattern of a word?
- Making up a rhyme or a mnemonic?
- Breaking words up into their constituent parts or identifying smaller words inside them?
- Knowing the derivation of a word?

Unit 28: Research words

Objective ·····>

- To secure the spelling of key terms and new words from across the curriculum.

Spelling Focus

- You may encounter some difficult words when you try to carr out research in a library.
- This unit will highlight a variety of ways to help you to spell and understand these words. These include:
  - looking for prefixes and word roots that will help you to investigate the derivation of the word
  - breaking the words into syllables and pronouncing each par
  - identifying smaller words in larger words
  - inventing mnemonics from the words
  - using the Look, Say, Cover, Write, Check spelling strategy.

  You don't need to use all these methods every time, but it is useful to have them available when you face a problem.

Starter >

1 Look at the commonly misspelled words in the Problem Box.

Problem Box
classification, irrelevant, section, series, system, article, editor, extract, summary, website, question, material

Divide the words into syllables and pronounce each part. Copy and complete the chart. Rewrite each word using the Look, Say, Cover, Write, Check spelling strategy.

Word	Syllables				
	1st	2nd	3rd	4th	5th
classification	cla	ssi	fi	ca	tion
irrelevant					
section					

Practice >>

2 Look for small words in the larger words below.

> copyright, catalogue, dictionary,
> glossary, librarian, content, magazine,
> reference, Internet, resource

Copy and complete the chart. Rewrite each word
using the Look, Say, Cover, Write, Check spelling
strategy.

Word	Smaller words I have found
copyright	copy, right, cop
catalogue	
dictionary	

3 Make mnemonics from the words you find.
For example: *It's not RIGHT to breach copyRIGHT.*

Extension >>>

4 Consider the words in the box below. Look for prefixes, suffixes or roots
which will help you with the derivation of the words. Use a dictionary to
help. An etymological dictionary will be even better.

> alphabetical, anthology, encyclopaedia, genre, index,
> photocopy, thesaurus, author, novel, publisher

Copy and complete the chart. Rewrite each word using the Look, Say,
Cover, Write, Check spelling strategy.

Word	Derivation	Other words I have found that use the same prefix, suffix or root
alphabetical	From 'alpha' and 'beta' – first letters of Greek alphabet	

5 Find other words that use the same
prefix, suffix or root as the words above.

Feedback ↩

Think about which of these help *you* most:
- The sound or the pattern of a word?
- Making up a rhyme or a mnemonic?
- Breaking words up into their constituent parts
  or identifying smaller words inside them?
- Knowing the derivation of a word?

Objective ·····>

- To secure the spelling of key terms and new words from across the curriculum.

Spelling Focus

- Many words in Maths come from the Ancient world where the subject was developed.
- This unit will highlight a variety of ways to help you to spell and understand these words. These include:
  - looking for prefixes and word roots that will help you to investigate the derivation of the word
  - breaking the words into syllables and pronouncing each part
  - identifying smaller words in larger words
  - inventing mnemonics from the words
  - using the Look, Say, Cover, Write, Check spelling strategy.

  You don't need to use all these methods every time, but it is useful to have them available when you face a problem.

Starter >

❶ Look at the commonly misspelled words in the Problem Box.

> **Problem Box**
> *adjacent, amount, approximately, corresponding, denominator, estimate, horizontal, kilometre, parallel, numerator, negative, perpendicular, radius, rotation*

Divide the words into syllables and pronounce each part. Copy and complete the chart. Rewrite each word using the Look, Say, Cover, Write, Check spelling strategy.

Word	Syllables				
	1st	2nd	3rd	4th	5th
adjacent	ad	ja	cent		
amount					
approximately					

Practice »

2 Look for small words in the larger words below.

> weight, addition, alternate, average, digit, divide, fraction, guess, isosceles, measure, percentage, questionnaire, recurring, irregular, subtraction

Copy and complete the chart. Rewrite each word using the Look, Say, Cover, Write, Check spelling strategy.

Word	Smaller words I have found
weight	eight
addition	

3 Make mnemonics from the words you find.
For example: **There's an EIGHT in wEIGHT.**

Extension »»

4 Consider the words in the box below. Look for prefixes, suffixes or roots which will help you with the derivation of the words. Use a dictionary to help. An etymological dictionary will be even better.

> angle, axis, calculate, centimetre, circumference, co-ordinate, decimal, diameter, equilateral, equation, kilogram, multiplication, perimeter, quadrilateral, subtraction, triangle, graph

Copy and complete the chart. Rewrite each word using the Look, Say, Cover, Write, Check spelling strategy.

Word	Derivation	Other words I have found that use the same prefix, suffix or root
angle	From Latin 'angulus' meaning 'corner'	

5 Find other words that use the same prefix, suffix or root as the words above.

Feedback ↻

Think about which of these *you* find useful:

- The sound or the pattern of a word?
- Making up a rhyme or a mnemonic?
- Breaking words up into their constituent parts or identifying smaller words inside them?
- Knowing the derivation of a word?

Objective ·····>

- To secure the spelling of key terms and new words from across the curriculum.

Spelling Focus

- Many words in Music come from other languages, particularly Italian.

- This unit will highlight a variety of ways to help you to spell and understand the variety of Music words. These include:

  – looking for prefixes and word roots that will help you to investigate the derivation of the word

  – breaking the words into syllables and pronouncing each part

  – identifying smaller words in larger words

  – inventing mnemonics from the words

  – using the Look, Say, Cover, Write, Check spelling strategy.

  You don't need to use all these methods every time, but it is useful to have them available when you face a problem.

Starter >

❶ Look at the commonly misspelled words in the Problem Box.

> **Problem Box**
> chromatic, crotchet, dynamics, lyric, major, melody, percussion, rhythm, synchronise, symphony, concerto

Divide the words into syllables and pronounce each part. Copy and complete the chart. Rewrite each word using the Look, Say, Cover, Write, Check spelling strategy.

Word	Syllables				
	1st	2nd	3rd	4th	5th
chromatic	chro	ma	tic		
crotchet					
dynamics					

Practice >>

2 Look for small words in the larger words below.

> *composition, conductor, harmony, instrumental, musician, orchestra, score, syncopation, chord, chorus, quartet*

Copy and complete the chart. Rewrite each word using the Look, Say, Cover, Write, Check spelling strategy.

Word	Smaller words I have found
composition	*position, posit*
conductor	

3 Make mnemonics from the words you find.
For example: *I always SIT down to write a compoSITion.*

Extension >>>

4 Consider the words in the box below. Look for prefixes, suffixes or roots which will help you with the derivation of the words. Use a dictionary to help. An etymological dictionary will be even better.

> *octave, choir, piano, ostinato, interval, quaver, semi-breve, tempo, ternary, timbre, triad, vocal*

Copy and complete the chart. Rewrite each word using the Look, Say, Cover, Write, Check spelling strategy.

Word	Derivation	Other words I have found that use the same prefix, suffix or root
octave	*From Latin meaning 'eight'*	
choir		

5 Find other words that use the same prefix, suffix or root as the words above.

Feedback ↩

Think about which of these *you* find useful:

- The sound or the pattern of a word?
- Making up a rhyme or a mnemonic?
- Breaking words up into their constituent parts or identifying smaller words inside them?
- Knowing the derivation of a word?

Published by Letts Educational
The Chiswick Centre
414 Chiswick High Road
London W4 5TF
Tel: 020 89963333
Fax: 020 87428390
email: mail@lettsed.co.uk
website: www.letts-education.com

Letts Educational Limited is a division of Granada Learning Limited, part of the Granada Media Group.
© Ray Barker and Louis Fidge 2002
First published 2002
ISBN 1 84085 665 3

British Library Cataloguing in Publication Data
A catalogue record for this book is available from the British Library.

Acknowledgements

The publishers would like to thank the following for permission to use copyright material. Every effort has been made to trace copyright holders and to obtain their permission for the use of copyright material. The author and publishers will gladly receive information enabling them to rectify any error or omission in subsequent editions.
Illustrations Tophams Picturepoint pages 56, 60, 62; Harry Bell pages 52 and 54

Commissioned by Helen Clark
Project management by Vicky Butt and Aetos Ltd
Editing by Diana Roberts and Jane Otto
Cover design by Bigtop Design .
Internal design by Aetos Ltd
Illustrations by Sylvie Poggio Artists Agency: Nick Duffy, Tony Forbes and Roger Langridge
Production by PDQ
Printed in the UK by Ashford Colour Press